SMILING MIND

Mindfulness Made Easy

SMILING MIND

Mindfulness Made Easy

**Jane Martino
& James Tutton**

We dedicate this book to the thousands of people—young and old—who use Smiling Mind and share our vision to spread the gift of mindfulness far and wide, making the world an even better place.

CONTENTS

1
Spreading the word on mindfulness

2
What is mindfulness?
page 16

3
The benefits of mindfulness

4
How to be mindful

SMILING MIND: AN INTRODUCTION

Hey! You might have picked up this book with a small amount of curiosity about mindfulness meditation. Well, we are not experts by any stretch, but we hope that actually helps unpack the mysteries even faster—we're Jane and James, the creators of Smiling Mind, a not-for-profit initiative designed to help as many people as possible connect with mindfulness meditation, at no cost to them.

Why did we do it? Because it has made such a big positive difference to our own messy lives, we wanted everyone to have the chance to experience it.

If you've never tried it before, mindfulness meditation can seem a bit intimidating. Don't worry, we've been there too—until we realised just how easy it was to get started.

Throughout this book, we're going to introduce you to the basics of mindfulness so you can start to enjoy some of the benefits we have over the years. We'll share the tips and tricks that we picked up along the way within our chaotic lives, as well as practical exercises to help your mind smile in no time.

Jane and James

SPREADING THE WORD ON MINDFULNESS

JANE SAYS:

Aren't we all just so busy, *all* of the time?

So often I catch myself answering a question like 'How are you?' with 'Oh, soooo busy, there's just so much going on at the moment,' like that is a good thing!

Life for most of us consists of incessant emails, phone calls, projects, school pick-ups and drop-offs, exercise, study, catching up with friends and family, sporting commitments, working hard to earn a living, birthday parties… and the list goes on.

All of this activity, seemingly connecting us with the world and each other, so often leaves many of us feeling, well, cold. We find ourselves fervently searching for connection as if it were the final prize in a treasure hunt and we're quickly running out of time. The irony is, connection is more often than not right in front of us. A meaningful exchange with a stranger, a long run on the beach, the chance to speak in front of hundreds of people—OK, that is probably more like a nightmare, but you get my drift.

We are so very busy that we miss the chance to marvel in the small things, and we miss the chance to stop and think about what we can do for others—all things which lead to a closer connection to others and to ourselves.

You see, meditation has made me a much better person, but not in a cliché, 'my life is soooo perfect' kind of way—quite the opposite, actually.

It has given me freedom.

I started meditating one day almost ten years ago because a friend suggested I try it. I am what my friends call 'a junkie for all things alternative health' (aka up for anything). I have had all kinds of needles in all kinds of places, drunk smelly green herbs and had complete strangers press trigger points and place hot glass jars on my back. So it seemed sitting in one place and repeating a mantra or listening to instructions would be a breeze.

Not so much. Apparently I was not that good at sitting still—and boy, was my mind busy. Although I was under strict instruction not to expect to awaken from my twenty-minute session as 'a new person', I could not help hoping for it. I found it hard, and I felt like I was never going to be able to have a clear mind.

Now that I know a little more about it, I realise most, if not all, of my meditation sessions may well be like this—and that is OK. The point is, I stick at it, I give my body and my mind that time and, like any form of fitness training, the more I do, the stronger my mind and ability to focus will be.

So how has meditation given me freedom? It has helped me to accept that I am not, and never will be, a perfect anything. It has woken me up to my behaviour, and what I want to change and try to do better. It has allowed me to cut myself some slack and admit I am doing my best, and that is about the only part that is perfect.

That's right. All you folks who were about to write me an email or post on social media that I am a fraud and no guru, because you saw me just last week yelling at my kids in the supermarket, don't bother. I already know—and my secret is already out. I'm imperfect, and I'm OK with that.

It was this acceptance of imperfection that compelled me to start Smiling Mind. I realised that perhaps there was a way I could help others slow down and give themselves 'a break', build healthy habits and a strong mind. Imagine if I had possessed this superpower in high school, at the start of my career or when entering parenthood? I wanted to help others experience what I had—but sooner.

The urgent need the world possessed became suddenly apparent and, like most things in my life, it just happened to be my business to make something happen—no point just thinking and talking about it! I've always felt action has been the secret to my success, so why would bringing mindfulness meditation to the masses be any different?

This book contains plenty more secrets—but the good kind. The ones that allow you to give yourself a break (yes, you are doing well), learn and enjoy switching on to your life, whatever it looks or feels like—warts and all.

PS: Just like real warts, you can burn them off, but some just keep growing back—so remember that as you read on!

JAMES SAYS:

I will start by sharing some basic facts about me and my meditation 'journey'.

First things first, I want to let you know that it's not like I sat down and meditated one day, was bathed in white light and have meditated for an hour every day ever since.

Like everyone else, I have good days, shit days and days when life is like being in a tumble dryer. But meditation has been wonderful, and it has slowly, but surely, become a habit. I still miss days, but I notice the absence now. I miss the calm. I miss that clarity. I miss the inner peace and love.

I should also point out that I am not a sage on a hill who has pursued a singular passion for meditation at the expense of a more conventional life. No, I'm a hands-on father, real-estate developer, entrepreneur and hopefully an active contributor to the broader community.

I was exposed to meditation at a young age, when I was at a wild and wonderful 'hippy' primary school called Preshil. In the afternoon we would lie down and put blankets over our legs and shoulders. We would close our eyes and just be still. It wasn't introduced to us as meditation; it was introduced to us as 'quiet time'. I instantly found it could take me to a happy place. Later on, with Smiling Mind, remembering that experience made me aware how easy it is to plant the seed of meditation in a young person. The door to meditation was opened for me when I was very young, which meant my return to it in my adult life was that much more natural.

In high school I was too busy being a ratbag to sit and meditate. I was every mother's worst nightmare—an encyclopedia of anti-social behavior. Things then started to shift at university, when I was studying philosophy, focusing on big ideas and questions. I started out meditating with some Buddhists occasionally, and I think from there something started to change—a little flame from my earlier years was alive and well.

For me, meditation is like learning to play guitar—you don't just pick up a guitar and play like Jimmy Page. It takes practice.

And once I started to enjoy the whole process of pausing, of slowing down, it then started to permeate my whole life and existence. It's not just about the moments in meditation; it's about taking the mindfulness that this meditation can ignite into your daily life.

There are times when I truly need to meditate. A 'sit' can put all my stresses into perspective. I have been known to turn off my phone and sneak out between meetings to meditate by the water. When I start, I can feel the pressure of phone calls, emails, commitments, schedules all pulsing through my body—the tension, the restlessness, that feeling of being rattled. I sit and breathe, or even lie down on a park bench (which can look ridiculous when you are six-foot-three). The mental traffic in my head begins to slow down, and pauses appear between the incessant thoughts. I start to notice silence. I can sense the fresh air, notice my breath and feel the tension leave me. I become calmer, kinder and ready to engage with the day.

My time meditating in the morning, before my family wakes, is some of the most substantial time in my day. This practice allows me to get off that roller-coaster of thoughts and pause, just sit.

Through finding mindfulness, I have been able to engage in life with more trust, confidence, an open heart and a smile. I can say, without reservation, that my journey with Janey to turn this crazy not-for-profit start-up into a success has been profoundly worthwhile for me as a person, for my family, for work, for my friendships and the wider community. I also have a heartfelt belief that as successful entrepreneurs who have benefited from our prosperity of our community, we are obliged to use our skills to do good in this world—Smiling Mind is a manifestation of that life view.

A Smiling Mind is something I will always want to cultivate. I still have my less mindful days, and I can still be a bit of a ratbag, but I know I am better for every minute that I spend in the remarkable state of mindfulness. If you embrace mindfulness, I promise, in time (and quicker than you may think) the world will smile back.

WHAT IS
MINDFULNESS?

So, what exactly do we mean by mindfulness?

Well, mindfulness is paying full attention to what is happening around you and inside you.

That is, in your body, heart and mind.

And doing this without criticism or judgement.

Mindfulness is about becoming aware of the present, noticing thoughts as they come and go, observing the breath and any other sensations.

And rather than getting attached to the thoughts that come into your mind, or expecting to feel a certain way, you stay open and aware in the present, allowing thoughts to pass like clouds. Mindfulness is not about feeling any particular way; it is about paying attention to right now. Often when we feel negative emotions, such as worry or anxiety, these are fuelled by thoughts of the past or worries about the future.

Mindfulness involves resting our mind in the present moment.

If you've never tried mindfulness meditation before, you might feel like you don't truly understand it, or you may be perplexed about how the hell you will add one more thing onto your already bulging daily to-do list. The reality is, it is actually very simple, requires no specialist skills, training or equipment—aside from your body and your mind, of course— yet will most likely be one of the most life-changing things you will try.

Life-changing how?

Well, we will get to that in more detail later, but in short—how does increased energy, better sleep, more empathy, higher levels of self-awareness and self-acceptance and a heightened ability to focus and be productive sound?

Even if this sounds worthwhile, you might not be sure where or how to start. That's where we come in, to reassure you it is best to just start, accept there will be challenges—as with anything worthwhile in life—and just keep going.

Start small and build from there. We like to call it 'bite size'—this makes it feel less like a mountain you cannot climb. We'll provide you with some short one-minute meditations, as well as other practices that will naturally increase the mindful moments in your day-to-day life. Then you will slowly feel ready and able to build up to the longer meditations. Remember, from little things, big things grow.

OMG, 60,000 THOUGHTS A DAY!

Here is some brain trivia for you.

The average brain generates somewhere up to 60,000 thoughts per day, more than forty thoughts every minute.

It is exhausting just thinking about that.

Once you start noticing the incessant chatter, you realise how relentless the mind can be. No wonder it is so hard to be present. Your mind is sending you to and fro, into the past, into the future. At Smiling Mind, we talk about having 'too many tabs open' at once—the tabs are all the thoughts about the past and future. We have only reflected on a minute here. What about an hour?

A whole day?

Sit and write down the string of thoughts that comes into your head over one minute.

Go on, time it.

Your mind may dart from thinking about putting the bins out, to making a phone call, wishing you were lying on the beach, sex, some business you need to look into, trying to remember the guy that is singing the song on the radio, looking up Instagram, or remembering to check in for a flight tomorrow, feed the dog, buy a birthday present, get petrol and put the gumboots in the car.

BREAKING THROUGH THE BARRIERS

We've heard it all before.

Mainly because it is exactly the same ridiculous bullshit we used to say ourselves.

'I am too busy to meditate.'

'I do yoga, and there is some meditation at the end of each class.'

'I am just not the type of person who likes to sit still, so meditation is not for me.'

And so on.

Yes, we are calling you on this—none of it is worth continuing to believe. Bust through these roadblocks!

A sense of relief awaits.

List five reasons why you don't have time to meditate.

Then take a breath and respond to each of these lame excuses.

JAMES SAYS:

Here's my list of excuses and responses, to show you how it looks.

1 **'I've tried it but it doesn't work on me.'**

There is no shining light or choir of angels. Rather, meditation is a slow thing—it takes a little time to form the habit and for the benefits to arrive. If you are struggling, then please, don't force it. Resist the urge to give up entirely, and gently try it again tomorrow.

2 **'I don't have time in the morning and I'm too tired at night.'**

There's a saying that if you don't have time to meditate for fifteen minutes, you should do an hour. I no longer tell myself I don't have time to meditate. I make time. I know plenty of people who even fit in sessions at work, in the car, etc.

3 **'I can't stop the thoughts.'**

This is probably a sign that you should meditate. If your mind is hyperactive when you are meditating, let it be active. Just stop fighting it. With practice, you will be able to allow your thoughts to come and go more freely.

4 **'I just don't think I am doing it the right way.'**

There is no one 'right way'. I can talk from personal experience: if you are struggling and feel you can't find 'the right way', you might want to start meditating with a focus on the breath (more on that shortly).

5 **'I'll never be that relaxed, calm meditator sitting in lotus position.'**

I'll let you into a secret; don't worry about the perfect state. That is a bit of a fantasy, actually. The state you are in, right where you are, is just fine.

EXERCISE
#3

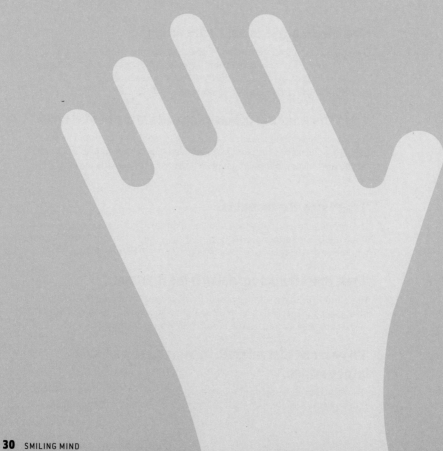

Now list five reasons to make time to meditate.

JANE SAYS:

Here's my list of reasons, to show you how it looks.

1

I feel more connected with those I love.

This is the most important. Human connection and a better connection with ourselves is something that makes life richer, simple as that.

2

I have more patience with others.

Whether you are running an empire of the residential or commercial kind, this is an essential ingredient to success in terms of relationships and productivity.

3

I am sharper.

My brain works better. I can feel it—more clarity and the ability to think and act more decisively and with added confidence.

4

Because I know it is good for me.

Kind of like holding my nose and drinking green smoothies or herbs the naturopath prescribed, I do not always have to be feeling or understanding the immense benefits meditation can bring. Research proves it, I can feel it myself most of the time—and that knowledge is more than enough for me.

5

I present better.

This may be a bizarre one to include, but for all of those out there petrified of public speaking (I hear it is up there with fear of death for most of us!), it really does work. Before every major presentation, interview or important meeting, I do a short five-minute meditation and it makes the world of difference to the way I feel in the moment and deal with nerves.

JAMES SAYS:

Here's my list of reasons to show you how it looks.

1 **To live in the present.**

One day you will notice that you are in the present—you will see a cloud in the sky, notice a smell or hear a sound and something will click. This is what being present and mindful is all about and it brings with it untold joy.

2 **To find stillness.**

One of my strongest character traits is a real restlessness—I can seem like I'm just about to make a run for it (likely to a warm beach). Meditation is incredibly grounding for me; I can come home to myself, stay put and find a tranquillity and stillness.

3
To give me a sense of playfulness.

One of the best things about meditation is that it can give us back our sense of fun. Play enables us to reconnect with a natural, more innocent state and not take life so seriously. Meditation has helped me to prioritise play—with my son at the beach, goofing around at a skate park, playing a game with my daughter and our dogs or just mucking around the house. It is a true joy in my life.

4
I am far nicer to be around.

I have had periods in my life when I was overly direct, very pushy, combative and entirely lacking in mindfulness and the empathy that goes with it. Meditation has really helped build my emotional awareness, which makes me less likely to be so reactive and more likely to be caring.

5
To seek peace.

Meditation has given me the ability to feel a sense of peace, something that had eluded me for a lot of my adult life. I think that this peace has come from letting go of the constant noise of the mind. I can now put that noise into the background and bring the breath to the foreground (a bit like noise-cancelling headphones for your brain).

YOU ARE READY, ANYTIME

Often, meditation guides create even more barriers by saying that we need to find a special place to do our meditation, wear comfortable clothes or take a bath or shower beforehand. All of these things can be valuable and quite possibly add to the meditation experience; however, they are not essential. And the last thing we need to be doing is adding more reasons for people not to meditate.

You might be the great unwashed, or sweaty from racing from one meeting to another, or just feeling frazzled after the witching hour is over and the kids are in bed. All of these are perfect times to meditate—however you are, wherever you are.

Life is unpredictable. Life is noisy. If we can build up the ability to stay with a meditation even through some distractions or external noise, then that can be a very positive thing.

Remember, there is no such thing as perfection, and that not only includes us as humans but how our meditation sessions should be or feel.

'Oh I cannot possibly meditate. I am not freshly bathed and sitting on my special cushion.'

JANE SAYS:

I have had some of my best meditations sitting in my car.

Often, if I have failed to wake up early enough to fit a session into my morning routine, I will get out my phone during the day—in the work car park or if I arrive early for a meeting—and play a ten-minute guided meditation while sitting upright in the driver's seat of my car.

I have even done this when parked on a main street and been sprung by a friend. She snapped a photo of me, and when I checked my phone following my meditation, there I was, a picture of me caught in the act! How good would it be if instead of a magazine article on 'Stars without make-up', there was 'Stars caught meditating'? That would be the point at which we knew meditation really was changing the world.

JUST
BREATHE

If you can breathe, you can be mindful. Bringing awareness and attention to your breath is one of the easiest ways to be mindful.

EXERCISE
#4

Start by making sure that your back is straight and that you're comfortable— you can be sitting or lying down.

Now close your eyes. If you are not comfortable closing your eyes, you can simply rest your gaze on one spot on the floor beneath you so your eyes are half-closed. Now place both hands on your stomach. Can you feel your hands moving with your breath?

As you breathe in, imagine your breath moving deep down into your stomach. Feel your hands rise as you breathe in, and fall as you breathe out.

You might notice that, while you try to pay attention to your breath, your mind wanders or gets distracted. This is completely normal. Every time you realise that your mind has wandered, gently bring your attention back to your breathing.

Try counting six breaths, feeling your stomach rise when you breathe in and fall when you breathe out. You have just meditated for one minute—how easy was that?

'Breathing in, I calm body and mind. Breathing out, I smile.

'Dwelling in the present moment I know this is the only moment.'

—Thich Nhat Hanh
Vietnamese Buddhist

THE BENEFITS OF MINDFULNESS

So this life-changing habit sounds helpful, but you do not have to just believe us.

There are decades (maybe even centuries) of research to show the positive changes that happen in our brains when we meditate regularly. Researchers have proven that meditation changes the brain and improves its volume in areas relating to emotion regulation, positive emotions and self control (ah, that's the smiling mind).

We've all heard in recent years about neuroplasticity—how the brain can actually change. Depending on the activities we choose to repeat, parts of our brain get enhanced or enlarged. A 2015 report by world-renowned neuroscientist Richie Davidson explains how the brain changes with meditation: 'We can intentionally shape the direction of plasticity changes in our brain. By focusing on wholesome thoughts, for example, and directing our intentions in those ways, we can potentially influence the plasticity of our brains and shape them in ways that can be beneficial.' Davidson goes on to say that even short amounts of meditation per day can change the brain.

Another great development has been how neuroscientists are beginning to understand and explain the 'monkey' (or restless) mind; meditators have been exploring this concept for centuries. Neuroscientists believe this incessant activity happens in a place in the brain called the default mode network (DMN). With regular meditation, the DMN decreases and is less active—something that scientists are able to measure.

Neuroscientists have also found that long-term practice of mindfulness alters the structure and function of the brain to improve the quality of both our thought and feeling. You see, when we get stressed, it triggers the 'fight or flight' response in our nervous system so that our bodies can react appropriately to danger. How clever is that?

What is not so clever is that we somehow have created lives where we activate this response on a consistent—if not constant—basis when we simply do not need it. When this response is activated, our body goes into survival mode: shutting off our digestive system, stopping growth and reproduction, and impairing our immune system. The survival mode should switch off when the 'threat' has subsided, but our modern lifestyles, thoughts and feelings of fear or anxiety are maintaining this response longer than required.

At this point, stress becomes detrimental to our mental and physical wellbeing. Studies at Harvard University have shown that mindfulness meditation decreases the stress response of the area in the lower brain that modulates stress levels (the amygdala) and activates those brain areas involved in emotional control. So mindfulness activates the relaxation response, helping to improve our physical and mental health, which of course is a wonderful and very important by-product of our investment in 'sitting' time.

Most crucially for us, it helps us focus and be in the moment, switching us on to every part of our life that the busyness had ensured we were brushing past, missing the wonder as we went.

Best part of it all? The whole process of mindfulness has the flow-on effect of making people more receptive and open—to themselves and other people.

A study conducted by Harvard researchers at Massachusetts General Hospital determined that meditation literally rebuilds the brain's grey matter in just eight weeks. One of the researchers, Sara Lazar, states that the research explains benefits far beyond stress relief and relaxation: 'Although the practice of meditation is associated with a sense of peacefulness and physical relaxation, practitioners have long claimed that meditation also provides cognitive and psychological benefits that persist throughout the day. Our study demonstrates that changes in brain structure may underlie some of these reported improvements and that people are not just feeling better because they are spending time relaxing.'

Medical science has started to uncover the extent to which mindfulness can help treat a range of mental conditions, from stress to depression. While most studies have focused on adults, more recent research shows mindfulness can also improve the mental, emotional, social and physical health and wellbeing of young people, which is an absolute game changer—allowing us to use these tools to address the mental health and wellbeing of our younger generations. That is, as long as we take up this healthy habit—and encourage friends, family and young people to do the same.

'Practitioners have long claimed that meditation also provides cognitive and psychological benefits.'

Just like eating well and exercising regularly, care for the mind is of equal importance.

Yet if we look at most parts of our society, especially the education system, it is the 'missing piece'. Hopefully, with a growing body of evidence and both popularity and belief in the practice of mindfulness meditation, it will be like the prodigal son who returns with much rejoicing and inclusion to be part of the family—and it will begin to feel as natural as if that part of ourselves, our health and daily routine never left in the first place.

The most important thing is: do not 'expect' anything and do not place pressure on yourself for your meditation to always be or feel a certain way. It is what it is and only through that attitude—trying a daily practice, falling off the wagon and getting back on it again—will we see and feel results.

Sometimes it is difficult to know whether the practice is really sinking in. Sometimes we get it straight away and start feeling the difference. Sometimes it can take quite a while and may feel like daydreaming. Sometimes you might continually fall asleep, but that does not mean it is not working or that you will never use and adopt the techniques over time. Most of the time we need to stop thinking about it or analysing it and just get started.

Mindfulness is a healthy habit in your toolkit of life. Unlike many of those we reach for (red wine, anyone?), this tool is a good one, because the more you do the better you feel (and behave).

One important note for those wanting to start a meditation practice or who might be experiencing intense emotional issues or thoughts when meditating: you could think about seeking further input from an experienced meditation teacher or experienced professional. Many psychologists and mental health organisations recommend mindfulness meditation as an important element of mental wellbeing.

If you feel like you need more help than mindfulness meditation can give, and need to talk to someone about where you are at, Lifeline, Kids Helpline and ReachOut.com are great places to start.

EXERCISE
#5

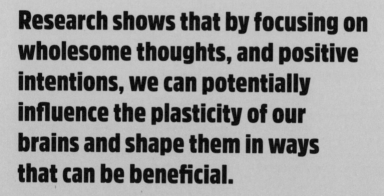

Research shows that by focusing on wholesome thoughts, and positive intentions, we can potentially influence the plasticity of our brains and shape them in ways that can be beneficial.

Often it can add an additional element to your meditation practice (and the incentive to keep it up!) if you create a positive intention to state at the beginning or throughout your meditation.

Here are some examples of positive intentions you might want to focus on as part of your mindfulness practice.

- I will practise being less judgemental.
- I will be mindful of needing to control every part of my life.
- If I feel overwhelmed by my thoughts, I can always come back to my breath.
- I will work on being less reactive to stressful situations. and be aware of my tendencies.
- I will practise kindness and gratitude.

JAMES SAYS:

I tend to create a positive intention by doing what Buddhists call a 'loving kindness' meditation.

I bring to my mind a moment of deep love: generally I picture myself lying in the sun with my daughter, and we're huddled under a beach towel laughing together. I then populate this image with my recollection of the smells, light and textures from that scene. Everything is reassembled to bring that moment of love back to me, and then I explore how I feel and let the love permeate my being and my meditation.

HOW MINDFULNESS CHANGES THE BRAIN AND BODY

We were astounded by the number of people who, when we talked about our idea to start Smiling Mind and take mindfulness meditation to the masses, thought it would never work.

To us, it was going to fill an urgent need for a pre-emptive health tool that did not always require human delivery methods nor did it have a cost associated. No-brainer, right?

Wrong.

People wanted proof.

So, we started on a long journey that led us to the cold hard facts. More than 2000 papers have been published in peer-reviewed journals showing meditation to have a positive effect on a range of stress-related illnesses, including but not limited to some of the studies we stumbled across below, which we want to share with you:

Heart disease, cholesterol and high blood pressure—these are eased as meditation evokes the 'relaxation response' (the opposite to the 'stress response'), lowering heart rate and boosting the immune system.

Insomnia—meditation can halve the length of time it takes someone with insomnia to get to sleep, according to research by Stanford University Medical Centre.

Anxiety and depression—the University of Massachusetts Medical School found a reduction in depression and anxiety in 90 per cent of patients with generalised anxiety disorder after eight weeks of meditating.

Psoriasis—the University of Massachusetts Medical School found meditators' skin cleared of the stress-related condition at four times the rate of those who didn't meditate.

Low fertility—an Oxford University study found stress can reduce the chances of women conceiving, and suggested meditation could be instrumental in combating a decline in fertility.

Stress—many studies show that practising mindfulness reduces stress. In one study at the University of Toronto, researchers found that participants who practised mindfulness-based stress reduction techniques had significantly less anxiety, depression and somatic distress when watching sad films compared with the control group.

As well as having positive effects on illness, mindfulness meditation can also enhance the healthy brain in the following ways:

Boosts to working memory—Improvements to working memory appear to be another benefit of mindfulness. A 2010 study by the University of Miami Psychology Department, for example, documented that the working memory capacity of a military group increased with meditation practice.

Focus—A study at the University of Liverpool examined how mindfulness meditation affected participants' ability to focus attention and suppress distracting information. The researchers found that experienced meditators had significantly better performance on all measures of attention than those with no meditation experience.

Relationship satisfaction—Several studies, including from the University of Rochester, find that a person's ability to be mindful can protect against the emotionally stressful effects of relationships.

Loneliness—Researchers at UCLA have found in a study that participating in an eight-week mindfulness-based stress reduction program reduced feelings of loneliness among older adults.

Social connectivity—At Stanford University's Centre for Compassion and Altruism Research, researchers conducted a two-month study to see whether meditation could impact how socially connected people feel. Participants were asked to practise meditations that centre on positive feelings of love and compassion towards the self and others. After two months, participants reported an increased sense of social connection in comparison to the control group.

Now, surely after all that, you do not need any more convincing that it is essential that you start a mindfulness meditation practice as soon as possible? And there is more research building by the day, which will soon enable us to see the practice permeate other areas of society where it is so desperately needed, such as workplaces, our healthcare providers and the justice and law enforcement system.

Mindfulness makes us better partners, parents and friends.

JANE SAYS:

One of the many great things for me about becoming more mindful was I quickly noticed it continuing to make me a better parent, partner and work colleague.

I first started meditating in the early years of parenthood, when I felt so sleep deprived yet still needed to slightly resemble a functional human being, I was willing to try anything.

Even without meditation, there is no doubt that parenthood has reconnected me to the parts of myself I had somehow buried over time. The importance of laughter, especially at myself, the wonder of 'the small things' and how hard it is to rush when you are genuinely being in the moment.

The combination of being mindful and being a parent is certainly powerful. However, I truly believe it does not take being a parent to appreciate the simple things, feel gratitude and, most importantly—connect with what truly matters and what it is that really makes your heart sing.

In my case it was simply starting to connect back with what I truly loved doing when I was younger. I always loved being a leader and received a great deal of joy and satisfaction from it—whether it was class rep, having a solo in choir or just taking charge of the chores on school camp, I'd happily jump in. This was no different at university or within the workforce. However, there was no comparison between the leader I was before and after I began meditating regularly.

Although I will always be a strong-willed and determined human (it's how I am wired, and I now am more accepting of that rather than critical, thanks also to meditation!), I now have far more empathy and understanding for those working alongside me, allow them to do things their way rather than insist on mine and have experienced far more success in business and as a 'boss' as a result.

JAMES SAYS:

I'm not shy to say it.
I used to be an arsehole.
I did things I am not proud
of—stupid things, which
my son would call
'dick moves'.

Mindfulness and daily meditation practice have changed me. I have gone from a pretty arrogant, hyper-aggressive, hyper-materialistic individual to someone who is not perfect but is far more caring and considerate—a person who actually wants to make a significant contribution to the world.

The more I have practised meditation, the more attention I have paid to thinking about the father I want to be and the more conscious my parenting has become. It means being less dismissive, less dogmatic and a hell of a lot more respectful.

As a side note, Smiling Mind was in some ways born from my own 'positive' midlife crisis. I asked myself if I was comfortable for my kids to see my contribution to this world along the lines of 'he developed big apartment blocks' (I work a lot in real-estate investment and development). The answer was 'no'.

Five years ago, if I had been dealing with my son's current chamber of dirty socks, unmade bed, school books all over the floor and those cords, wires and guitars to step over, I think about how incredibly frustrated and stressed I would have been about it. Now I am not getting stuck on those things.

For me, mindfulness facilitates a far higher level of acceptance of my children as individuals, as unique people, as opposed to seeking that they each become a mini-me. In the long term, I think this means they can grow up to be themselves, rather than growing up trying to please my vision of what they should or should not be.

That level of acceptance is also something I see in other relationships in my life. Mindfulness has enabled me to have more diverse friendships and deepen existing relationships. It has made me so much more open-minded, a better listener and more appreciative to conversation and connections with all ages, all political persuasions and all shapes and sizes.

I make a point of meeting new people all the time. Each week, I have coffee with new people just to ensure my world remains open. These meetings have led to some great business projects, diversified and strengthened my professional and personal networks and created opportunities for growth.

Practising mindfulness has also given a great depth and richness to relationships with my family members and colleagues. Mindfulness can switch on our capacity for empathy (and hence lasting positive connections). I am far more conscious if someone is not going well—and I will follow up with a phone call, send a text message, or buy them a bunch of flowers, a drink or a coffee. I am so much more likely to want to make those gestures than I was in the past. And I am far more likely to notice and appreciate kindness when it comes my way.

People can see karma as a mystical rebirth kind of thing, or they can see it as a very practical 'now' thing. I see it as a practical 'now' thing, and the plain truth is that if you engage with the world showing mindfulness, love and empathy, the world will show you a lot more of the same.

'I've learned that people will forget what you said, people will forget what you did, but people will never forget how you made them feel.'

—*Maya Angelou*
Author, poet and civil-rights activist

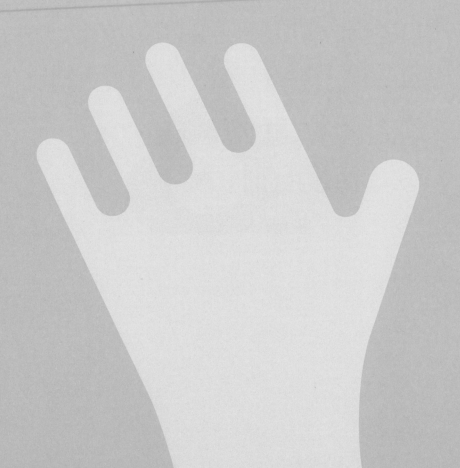

EXERCISE
#6

List five benefits of cultivating mindfulness in your life.

JANE SAYS:

Here's my list of benefits, to show you how it looks.

1

Coping better.

There is no doubt this is the number-one thing I have noticed since I started meditating. So much so, whenever I fall 'off the wagon' and do not meditate regularly I experience a noticeable difference in my ability for things to bother me… or not.

2

Noticing things others don't.

I don't mean this in a competitive way, but because you are more focused on being 'in the moment', you simply notice and take pleasure in the 'smaller things', and you seek out lots of special gestures and experiences that make life grand.

3

Feeling things more —or less.

Meditation makes you more empathetic and tuned in to your feelings and those of others. Do not panic, you won't become a blubbering mess, you will simply be more aware of how you are feeling and therefore be able to address it accordingly. This also means you will be able to 'let go' more easily and not hang on to negative feelings as you may have in the past.

4

Increasing your energy levels.

They say twenty minutes of meditation is equivalent to more than triple that amount of shut-eye—and I believe it as there is a noticeable difference between my energy levels when I do and don't meditate regularly.

5

Being more in tune with your body.

For me and my 'I need to conquer the world' tendencies, this is an important gift that meditation has bestowed—it allows me to know when to stop, slow down or simply address any health issue I sense may be brewing. This is crucial in keeping my batteries charged.

JAMES SAYS:

Here's my list of benefits, to show you how it looks.

1

Stress busting.

I find that if I don't meditate and cultivate mindfulness in my day, I do enter a world of the 'monkey mind'. When I'm stressed out, I get caught up in my own thoughts. That's when I describe my mind as a revolving to-do list that forgets to do everything. I can lose my cool and my modus operandi can leave a lot to be desired.

2

Being present.

If there is one reason alone to give mindfulness a try, it is to be more present with people you love, to be in the moment and able to give your loved ones the attention they deserve. Mindfulness makes me a more loving father, partner, friend and business guy.

3
Making friends with yourself.

My experience in life is that the first step towards peace with the world is making peace with yourself—it's like an oxygen mask on a plane: you need your own mask on before you help those around you—and acceptance, self-love and awareness come through mindfulness.

4
Dealing with uncertainty.

This is a really big one for me. With mindfulness, I am no longer constantly looking for the quick answer and instant 'solution'. I'm less likely to say, 'I am absolutely certain about that.' I accept now that uncertainty is the only certainty we have. It doesn't mean I don't make plans, but I no longer hold the deluded belief that I can be certain about how things are going to turn out.

5
Noticing the little things (and they become big things).

It might sound corny, but mindfulness does make little things in life really wonderful. For me it's the first coffee of the day; it's the special spoon I always put out with my daughter's porridge, with her favorite bowl; it's morning sunshine. If you practise mindfulness, you will notice really remarkable things. You find out the things that you really value, as opposed to blindly going about your day chasing things that society says you should value.

HOW TO
BE MINDFUL

By now you must be thinking— well, this all sounds good, and fairly logical, but how do I do it?

How can I bring a sense of mindfulness into my everyday life?

There are many ways to do this—and we will share lots of them in the rest of this book.

However, one of the most powerful ways to cultivate mindfulness is to set aside ten to twenty minutes each day to practise mindfulness meditation.

Finding this time may at first seem challenging but that is just an excuse not to start. Trust us—we were both guilty of that! It actually is quite simple to find the time, especially once you see how much it transforms and improves the way you think and feel about yourself, others and the world around you.

Studies show that even after ten minutes a day for ten consecutive days you should start to see and feel some positive changes. This is simply because a regular mindfulness meditation practice reminds us not to waste mental energy taking visits to the past or future but to keep ourselves exactly where we are at this very time, which is much more relaxing for our mind and body.

'The mind is like a parachute, it does not work if it is not open.'

—Frank Zappa
Musician, songwriter, composer, and record and film producer

At times, people get confused because they expect things with big impact to be complex.

Well, guess what? That's not how meditation works. It's simple and it's big impact.

What's more, Smiling Mind has made meditation and mindfulness even simpler by ensuring it's free to access and always close at hand (on your phone!). What was once a simple thing that might have been tricky to find is now a simple thing available free on the breadth of digital platforms.

Here are the basics.

Start where you are

Meditation might be a completely new experience for you, or it might be something you have been toying with off and on for a while. It does not matter. Just start where you are, not where you wish you were or where your friend the yogi is with their practice. It is vital not to stress, whatever happens during the practice. Even the most experienced meditators have sessions where it's really hard to settle.

Repeat this mantra: Don't stress. Don't stress. Don't stress. All you have to do is breathe, relax and let the thoughts subside.

Work out what works for you

Sit, lie down, even walk—there are many different ways to meditate, so find out what works for you. It's crucial to be comfortable and to be able to stay awake. It is also important to adopt an aligned posture.

This means if you sit cross-legged when you meditate, the idea is to have your knees touching the ground for greater support. A pillow or bolster under the bottom can help tilt the pelvis and move the knees closer to the ground. If your knees don't touch the ground, use folded blankets or cushions to support them.

You can also use a meditation bench, which allows meditators to sit elevated in a kneeling position without pressure on the hips or joints. This handy little stool can also help with posture, making it a little easier to keep the spine straight (which helps with breathing properly too).

Those with back problems can choose to meditate in a chair, making sure that feet are not crossed and are resting flat on the floor, or to lie flat. The key thing is to keep the spine nice and straight and make sure you are comfortable. Some meditators think of a line or cord from the top of the head all the way down the spine and work to keep that beautifully straight, allowing the breath to flow up and down that centre line.

Another handy tip is to adjust the chin down a little bit so that your head is not leaning back. This can make a real difference to alignment. (Don't worry, the more you meditate, the more you will learn all sorts of little tweaks to the way you like to sit. You just know when it feels right.)

It is always good to take a few breaths to settle into the posture and make any adjustments before you begin the meditation practice. You will often see a seasoned meditator do a few stretches (like a swimmer before a race), shrug the shoulders and do a few shoulder rolls to help relax into position. Flex and relax. It can also help to consciously relax tension in the jaw too by opening and closing the mouth—up and down and side to side. It's amazing how much tension we hold there.

The breath

A beautiful part of meditation is observing the breath. Your mind will wander (this is what the mind does) but every time the mind darts off, bring your attention back to the breath. Just keep bringing attention back to the breath, over and over. Slowly but surely a new habit will form. Mindfully let any feelings of frustration or 'dammit' come and go.

Try to be curious as you explore your breath. Some people like to observe the breath in the nostrils as it goes in and out and will always come back to doing this if thoughts get too distracting. Others like to put a hand on the belly and feel the draw of breath up and down the torso. Starting off with a few deeper breaths can also set you up to shift into a more meditative space before you let the breath return to a more natural rhythm.

Explore how your breath changes throughout the day.

How is it when you wake up in the morning? How about when you are playing a sport or running around outside? What is it like when you're sitting in class concentrating on a challenging task? How is your breath when you're laughing hysterically?

When you are sitting in a room, on a bus, or in any other public space surrounded by people, look around and observe how everybody is breathing. Can you imagine how many people in the world are breathing in when you breathe in? Observe how you are breathing and feel the sensation—can you observe anyone else breathing mindfully?

You can check in with your breath a few times a day by asking yourself: 'Am I still breathing?' You might be surprised at how easy it is to forget to provide our body (and mind) with deep, clear breaths. We often hold our breath during the day without even realising it, when we're concentrating intensely or under pressure.

Be curious as you explore your breath and notice how it changes over the day or during different activities. A great way to remember to do this is by connecting it to a ritual activity you do several times a day, such as opening a door, sitting down or stopping at a traffic light if you do a lot of driving. Every time you do any of these things that are so automatic, you also do a quick check-in with your breath.

When to do it

We encourage you to develop a regular meditation practice. From our experience, it can help to formally set aside the time to do it, even diarise it if necessary; otherwise, if your days are anything like ours, time will run away and it will just become a stressful task on your to-do list.

It is also good to set aside a special place in your home, garden, workplace, car or suburb that you practise in. Pick a place where you are unlikely to be interrupted and explain to your family/housemates/work colleagues that it's best not to disturb you during the practice. They will get used to it—we promise. Some might even join you!

Tools and props

If you see a group of seasoned meditators on retreat, you will find that there are so many different ways to meditate.

Some will be sitting without any props; others will have cushions and bolsters under knees and bums; others will be sitting on little wooden Zen stools or meditation benches; some are cross-legged, others are kneeling; some will be meditating on a large pile of cushions and blankets; others will be on chairs, leaning against a wall or lying flat on their backs.

Some drape themselves in blankets, some sit on sheepskins; others use incense, candles and flowers as cues to enter meditative states. You need to find what works for you—it might be none of the above, and that is completely fine. The goal is to create the right space, the right posture, the right ambience for your practice. Don't get too fussy about it. It is about closing your eyes and letting go.

What is your style?

There are myriad styles of meditation—with mantras, chanting, silent, guided meditations, group meditations, so many different flavours.

Technology has opened up many new ways to meditate too—through apps like Smiling Mind; through podcasts with leading teachers around the world; through YouTube, subscriber websites and social media feeds. It really is a case of trying and testing different styles until you find what you like and what works for you.

Within Smiling Mind, we offer different approaches for different age groups. Some Smiling Minders like a body scan meditation; others prefer exercises with the breath; guided meditations; some with music; some without. It's all about finding your own sweet spot.

You will know when you have found the right method for you. You will tap into a miraculous well of stillness, of openness, of quiet calm and freedom.

Along with your breath, your body serves as a perfect object for your meditation because it is always there. (Have you ever left the house and realised that you've forgotten to take your body with you?)

So choose a point at the beginning of the day and one at the end of the day, and try to notice if your body feels different in the morning and the evening.

You can try tuning into your body twice a day for a very quick one-minute body scan.

It is easiest to do this one-minute exercise while sitting in a chair with your feet uncrossed and flat on the floor.

Take a minute to settle into your chair and allow your attention to move to your toes. If it's hard to feel your toes then wiggle them slightly. Feel the soles of your feet against the floor, then move up the body, feeling your ankles, calves, knees and thighs. Feel both of your legs resting against the chair. Notice if you are holding any tension anywhere in your legs and feet.

Now move your attention to your hands. Feel your thumbs and fingers, the palms of your hands, your wrists, arms and shoulders. Notice both arms and shoulders, becoming aware of any tension that you might be holding here.

Then move your attention to your belly and chest. Feel them expand and contract with your natural breath. Feel your back resting against the chair. Move your attention up your neck, your jaw, tongue, nose and eyes. Notice if you're holding any tension anywhere in your face. Then allow your attention to expand, noticing your whole body, sitting in the chair.

This is a great exercise to undertake in bed when you first wake up or when you're winding down after a big day—or even before you start your ten-minute guided meditation!

PRACTISING
MINDFULNESS

5

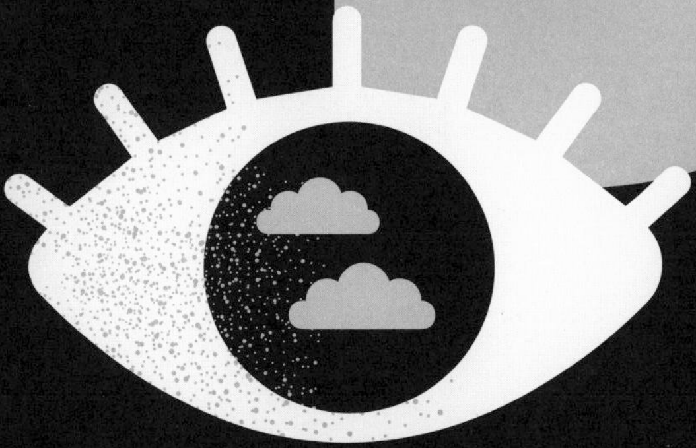

Welcome to the present

You might find that when you sit down to practise your daily meditation, you don't really seem to experience any particular emotion. Then later, when you're caught up in your emotion, you forget to bring mindfulness to the experience.

That is perfectly normal. It is only after regular practice that you start to bring the two together. As your self-awareness increases, you will find yourself identifying certain emotions as they arise. To bring awareness to your emotions while you are experiencing them, try the following exercise.

EXERCISE
#9

This is a very simple but eye-opening exercise in how powerful it is when we separate ourselves and our actions from our emotions—it does not mean we will no longer feel them, but simply that we will recognise and acknowledge the emotion. This will make us better equipped to react in a more positive way and change some behaviours over time that may be in fact contributing to the way we are feeling.

Close your eyes, take a few deep breaths and think back to a situation that made you really happy.

Try reliving that experience in as much detail as possible. Think about the people involved, the smells, sounds and sights.

As you do this, explore the sensations that arise in your body. Where do you feel your happiness or excitement?

Keep your attention on the sensations in your body and observe what happens when you do this.

Now imagine a situation that made you sad or angry, and do the same thing. Try reliving it in as much detail as you feel comfortable with.

Explore the sensations in your body, and how these sensations are different from the ones you experienced when you invoked the feelings of happiness.

Explore what happens when you observe your sensations while trying not to identify with the emotion.

To practise present-moment mindfulness:

Set a timer for sixty seconds. Settle into your preferred meditation position.

Close your eyes and become aware of the floor below you, supporting you. Find your centre, take three deep inhalations and exhalations, then return to more relaxed breathing.

Simply sit and observe what is happening in the moment.

Resist the urge to overthink what is happening. Just observe. Let thoughts come and go, and keep going back to the breath.

Each day, add an extra minute to this simple practice until you reach twenty minutes.

MINDFULNESS IN DAILY LIFE

One of the greatest challenges in building a meditation and mindfulness practice is how to do it within the context of busy lives—whether it's children to raise, demanding work lives, relationships to nurture or anything else.

Think of the times when you have arrived back from a fantastic holiday, all relaxed. You open your emails and within five minutes, the tan is fading, the pulse is racing and the stress is building. This is the exact time to become conscious of your reactivity and work on your mindfulness practice—it's the juncture between a moment of peace and the abyss of stress.

Instead of creating a story all about stress, why not just breathe, stay calm and stay mindful moment-to-moment, without jumping to conclusions that your world is falling apart because you had to leave the holiday behind? How? Simply take a moment to breathe and be in the present, or if the opportunity allows, take the time to sit and meditate and walk back from the habits which don't support a mindful life.

Mindfulness can be practised more formally via a guided mindfulness meditation as we have been exploring. However, there are lots of really great ways you can practice the art of being mindful more informally in everyday life just by taking an activity or daily ritual and truly paying attention.

Your 'mindful mate' could be anything from brushing your teeth to cooking dinner or playing a musical instrument—it means that you do these tasks, normally performed on autopilot, and use all your senses to be fully aware of what you are doing. For example, when brushing your teeth—really feel the bristles of the brush on your teeth and gums, hear the sound it makes, taste the toothpaste on your tongue and feel the breath coming in and out of your nose while you brush. Just like when you are meditating, your mind will wander off, but in a similar way, bring it back to focusing on the senses whenever you become aware of this occurring.

You will probably notice more than you ever have before—imagine how awake to our whole lives we can become if we take this example of mindful awareness into our relationships, conversations and even tasks at work!

SOME 'MINDFUL MATES' TO TRY

Walking

Walking meditation can be an absolute joy. The beauty of walking meditation is that you get lots of opportunities to practise it. This means you can bring mindfulness into your day at any time you happen to be walking for plain old functional reasons (like getting from A to B).

Think about creating a mindfulness of movement and consciously slowing down to be in the present moment. Focus on your feet and how they make contact with the ground. Take a step. Wait in anticipation for the sensation of touching the earth as the foot lands. You become mindful of the foot as it moves through the process of walking, up and down, up and down. Try and hold your focus gently on the movement of the lower body, including the feet and the legs. As a rhythm forms it becomes like the breath, a natural, rhythmic cycle.

Eating

We can all be emotional eaters—filling ourselves mindlessly with no heed to physical hunger. Eating mindfully is a wonderful way to ensure that we are getting the most from our food—the taste, the texture, the smell. It also brings us to reflect on how the food came about, who made it, who grew it, how processed it is (though it does make eating junk hard!). Mindful eating also serves to connect us to a whole-body approach to food as opposed to just consuming based on the cravings in our head. If we are mindful of our body's true hunger, and we go about eating slowly and mindfully, we are less likely to overeat.

You could start by smelling the food and looking at it—ask yourself, 'How did this come to my table?' Take smaller bites, look for texture, move your tongue around the food, feeling it against your gums and teeth. Chew more, pause more. It makes you realise how much we eat with very little thought.

Swimming

Water is beautiful—there is no life without water, and its presence against our bodies is a sensual experience, which is amplified if we move into and through water with mindful presence.

Before you enter the water—be it a pool or the ocean—try walking mindfully towards the point of entry, and when going in, see if you can enter slowly and feel the water contact the body and slowly creep up, inch by inch, as you submerge. Each part of the body will feel the water slightly differently, and as the head goes under, the awareness of holding one's breath increases. Sit still under the water to see what you can feel, what you can see. It can be very cleansing.

Washing

Your time in the shower can often be mindless. Why not start to really feel the water on your body, the sensations of bathing. Consciously smell the ingredients of your bath products. Washing also brings awareness to the whole body. With mindful washing, you create a ritual of cleansing until every nook and cranny is clean. Again, it is about turning a routine into a ritual.

Cooking

Mindful cooking is something that is often practised at retreats. It can feel very weird at first, chopping in slow motion, washing the lettuce with care… but it quite quickly becomes a really cool experience. It's like you are doing the task for the first time.

Notice the sensations of a knife as it cuts through the vegetables, as you add salt to the pasta pot. Like mindful eating, mindful cooking also gets you more in touch with the food you are eating. It's about switching on all your senses and really paying attention to the experience.

In meetings

Meetings can be messy—especially in workplaces where the culture is one of people not being clear on what they are seeking, having responses in their heads before others have stopped speaking, where dogma rules, and ideology and self-identity dictate how people respond to issues. It does not need to be that way.

Start by having everyone sit down. Agree on what the desired outcome is; agree on the mindful rules of engagement (no interruptions, focused listening, keep to the topic or at least acknowledge when moving away from it). If you feel it's right, start the meeting with a meditation—this calms people and lets the energy of the day dissipate. Being mindful is about focus, and an essential outcome of a mindful meeting is for everyone to walk away with some clear actions. There are times when there needs to be more thought given to the issues, but if that's the case, ensure the time frame and responsibilities are clear.

Driving

It's clear what happens if we are not mindful on the road—we can hurt ourselves and others. Hence, being a mindful driver is not just about improving our own wellbeing, it's about a responsibility to our community to act in a safe manner.

Sitting in one small space provides the ideal situation to connect the mind with the body. Put your hands on the wheel and look for tension, in your arms, your back, your stomach. Ask yourself, 'What's my internal weather doing?' Don't seek to change it, but acknowledge it.

When greeting someone

Pay attention—look into their eyes, engage and take the time and respect to understand how they feel, both via their words and through subtle non-verbal cues. If we are to greet people mindfully, we need to listen for not just what has been said but what has not been said. Simple things like smiling, using people's names and sincere compliments all help build mindful connections when greeting. If people are coming into your space, it's the small things. Light candles, have flowers, offer drinks, be an attentive host. These small things add up and help build warmth and love between people.

Listening

Too many people just don't listen. If you don't listen, you don't learn, and you are missing opportunities to mindfully build positive energy between you and the person talking. Focus your brain, body and soul on the other person's words and actions. Try not to drift away. Gently bring your focus back if you've started to drift into thoughts of the past or the future. This is not just an area of mindfulness reserved for a social context but also applies to our work and professional context. In fact, it applies to how we greet the person making our coffee or selling us our next house.

It is always good to go back to the basics of active listening:

- Seek to understand before you seek to be understood.
- Be non-judgemental.
- Give your undivided attention.
- Use silence effectively.

Observing

Too much of our physical and emotional world goes unobserved. One thing you can try to help make the seemingly mindless moments mindful is to take your focus away from what is obvious. When you walk down a street, shift your eyes above the streetscape to see what is on the horizon, what is above the shop fronts, what materials make up the buildings. It is even better in nature. Look for different greens in the trees, notice the shades. Feel the wind—how does it hit the trees, how do they move? The same applies with water: look for the shades of blue, and how the light changes it.

EXERCISE
#11

You can use sounds as the object for your meditation.

The sense of hearing and listening to something attentively and curiously is a great way to connect with the present moment.

Try listening to a song that you love. It could be one that you've heard many times before and know all the lyrics to. Try noticing five things about this song that you've never noticed before. How does this change the experience of listening to the song? Some people say it makes it more interesting and enjoyable.

If you like this exercise, you can make it a little more challenging and listen to a song that you do not enjoy. Try noticing five new things about it. See if you can find at least one thing about it that you enjoy. Exercises like this are great ways to practise being mindful but also to train ourselves to look for the positive!

JANE SAYS:

I often ask my children to really listen to a song and name all the instruments they can hear.

This truly invokes the senses and listening skills and becomes a fun, mindful game—especially on long car rides when three kids are in the back seat struggling to keep their hands to themselves!

EXERCISE
#12

Take a moment to connect with the feeling of your feet grounded firmly on the floor.

Place your awareness on the soles of your feet. Become aware of the sensations on the bottom of the feet such as the pressure of the ground beneath or the warmth of your socks and shoes. You might like to imagine you are wearing heavy 'moon boots' (or 'earth boots', really) that are keeping you heavily connected to the earth. By simply bringing your attention to your feet, you are reconnecting with this present moment. This is a really good, simple task to do if you start to feel a little upset or anxious.

JAMES SAYS:

Rituals are good and rituals can be bad.

It's good to use mindfulness to try and become more aware of good habits and bad habits. For the good rituals and habits, it means we are awake to them, we enjoy and respect the moment and perform those tasks in a state of heightened awareness, alive to the moment.

This, for me, brings joy to what was maybe a mundane 'auto-pilot' moment. For those rituals which are bad, the bad habits, mindfulness can help make us aware of them. How do we greet our friends, how do we listen to children, how do we show gratitude to our parents? By being mindful we have the ability to step back and fine-tune our reactions.

'If we make friends with ourselves, then there is no obstacle to opening our hearts and minds to others.'

—*Pema Chodron*
Notable American figure in Tibetan Buddhism

'SWITCH ON' TO YOUR LIFE

Once you start practising mindfulness, you'll discover that you can apply it to every part of your life.

Here are some ideas for how you can use mindfulness to 'switch on' your awareness and start experiencing kindness and compassion wherever you go.

BE IMPERFECT, IT'S LIBERATING

And not just for you! One of the most important benefits mindfulness can bring is the idea of acceptance. This naturally provides us relief from the expectations we put on ourselves to be a certain way.

We're not talking about being apathetic but simply giving yourself a break, cutting yourself some slack now and then.

JANE SAYS:

I talked about 'warts and all' earlier, and one thing that I have realised since starting to meditate is:

No matter how hard I try (and believe me, I do) nothing will ever be perfect, especially not me!

So take this challenge with me. Choose something you normally do not like, something that might irritate you about yourself, a situation or others. It might be someone leaving the toilet seat up every time (OK, I admit, with three sons that is on my list!); maybe it is people not letting you merge in traffic; it might be wanting the house to be a certain way or missing a gym session because you would prefer to sleep in. None of these things are ideal, but they are also not life-threatening. What is more life-threatening is getting upset about them or placing unnecessary pressure on yourself or others because of your set expectations.

Now, try for one week not to say anything about the messy house, don't worry if someone does not let you into their lane—the next guy will—and if you hit snooze one day, don't beat yourself up about it, just make sure you go to the gym the next morning. See if you can feel the difference in your body and levels of tension throughout the day.

Not only is this a great way to identify the things that might not really matter as much as you think they do, it will surprise and delight the people around you (especially the boys who are incessantly nagged about leaving the toilet seat up!).

EXERCISE
#13

List five things that stress you out to let go of this week.

JAMES SAYS:

This is by no means an easy list for me as I'm an obsessive person—my shoes are polished, my shirts are pressed, my teeth are flossed, my feet are pedicured.

Do I sometimes just let all these things fall in a heap? You bet. There are days when I just don't bother, and I don't feel the slightest bit guilty about it.

Seriously, do I need my feet any cleaner than they get in the shower? No. Does it matter that my car is full of my kids' snotty tissues? Not really. I'm not saying we should all live like sloths, but I definitely want to challenge myself to say, 'Let go for a week—it does not matter.'

My little list looks something like this…

1. **Checking my emails**
   Do you really need to respond that quickly?

2. **Cleaning my car**
   It will go from A to B if it's dirty or clean.

3. **Making the bed**
   It's just as warm if it's made or not.

4. **Cooking a fancy dinner**
   Sure, it is a lovely and rewarding thing, but not if you've blown all your energy and just need to lie down.

5. **Flossing your teeth**
   Surely they are clean enough just being brushed twice a day.

GIVE SOMETHING THAT REALLY MATTERS

Instead of a purchased gift for a friend for an upcoming birthday or special occasion, write them a letter. It can be as long or short as you like.

Express something you are grateful to them for as well as something you think they are great at.

JANE SAYS:

Here is a letter I wrote a friend instead of giving her a Christmas gift last year, and she said it was the best gift she had ever received.

As you know, this year I was insistent on not supplying anything material as a gift at Christmastime. Not because I am not fond of showering you with gifts or showing you I care by buying you something I know you will love and treasure, but because if I have learnt anything this year it is that sometimes it is the simplest and most honest things which not only mean so much but do so much.

So this is my gift to you. An honest account from me to you of what I am grateful for, how much you inspire me and what I want for you in 2015. There is much I am grateful for in my life; however, what I am most grateful for is the resilience and tenacity I possess to keep going even when things are challenging. Sometimes I am not quite certain where it was derived from or how I keep finding its source— but somehow I do. Then I look at you and am constantly inspired by everything you do, how you live your life and the resilience and strength you consistently show in times of absolute grief and despair. It seems to far outweigh anything I have ever witnessed.

It has been astounding for me to watch this strength, and I know many others around you have watched this, learned from it and become better people for it. Your sense of gratitude for the things you do have is so important and hearing you consistently come back to that inspires me to do the same.

Your willingness to hear me out and listen to my woes, which are so often insignificant compared to yours, is something, on reflection, I feel embarrassed by, but you never once make me feel anything but that 'you have my back' and understand how I am feeling.

Your ability to try new things, seek out adventure and challenge and totally review and change the direction of your life is pure joy to watch. It has already paid off greatly and I know will continue to as you use your newfound passion and skills to help make the world a better place.

I am grateful for all these wonderful qualities you possess and even the ones you have that are not so great—as they teach me plenty as well, and I have learnt to take the good with the bad and love you anyway, as have you. I am grateful for our friendship, its consistency and the love and laughter that is at the centre of it.

I am grateful for the end-of-the-day phone calls that put us both in a better place. I am grateful for the love and care you show each member of my family. I am grateful for the admiration for me you so freely give, even when it is barely deserved, and that no matter what, you think I am clever and special and you are always genuinely happy if and when I succeed.

So my Christmas wish for you is simple. Keep being grateful, keep being resilient, keep staying true to your hopes and passions—just keep doing the amazing job of life that you are. And my wish is that you will always be grateful for that.

List five people you need to write a thank-you note to in the next week and why.

JANE SAYS:

Visit someone in hospital.

I did this recently with my kids, who are seven, eight and nine. It was a long drive to see an elderly woman with no family and few friends. Little did the kids know, she was my library teacher when I was in primary school. Come to think of it, she was probably one of the first and most influential mindfulness teachers I have had—giving me my passion for reading and being 'in the moment' with a great book, a truly mindful experience.

We arrived and she was totally unable to move, and the pain medication she was on meant the boys witnessed her vomit rather than speak for the first fifteen minutes of our visit.

This experience meant the drive home was full of questions and provided an often-needed recalibration around how to show others you care, what is truly important and how very lucky we are to have healthy bodies (and minds!).

List five random acts of kindness —and complete them this week.

JAMES SAYS:

❶ Open the door and fill their glasses.

It is such an easy thing to do, so open the door for people, let people out of the elevator, be gracious. Similarly, whether you are hosting a dinner or simply having a meeting in a cafe, fill people's glasses—it's a simple thing, but it makes people feel at ease and shows you have their needs on your mind.

❷ Smile.

It's not rocket science—a smile makes people feel good. You radiate positive energy and people feel it. Look them in the eye, let your face light up and you'll find their face shines too. Young people, old people, men, women. Think of yourself as a politician—but a politician working for love, not the political left or the right. Your smile spreads love.

❸ Give support—unconditionally.

Too many people just don't do things for others unless they feel there is something in it for them. Well, my experience is that if you give others support, have a coffee with the person who reached out to you on LinkedIn, send a book to the friend of a friend who you heard is having a tough trot— these things all add up and they make for a better world.

❹ Write an email.

It could be the person who showed you a car, the parent of your kid's school friend, the assistant who arranged your meeting with their boss—it does not matter who they are, if people have been nice, say so. Even if they didn't seem that nice, say thank you anyway, because a little digital smile from you might be what they need to bring them back.

❺ Compliment a stranger.

You may feel it's cheesy or insincere, but if you see someone wearing a hat and you like it, just say it. I still remember being twenty-one and living in New York, and men and women there would just come out and say, 'Love that hat, brother.' Say it like it is and don't be shy. Where's the downside?

'No act of kindness is ever wasted.'

—*Aesop*
Ancient Greek storyteller

SWITCH OFF
SO YOU CAN SWITCH ON

Put your phone in the cupboard for a whole day over the weekend. Do not check it until after 5pm—or if you feel like being really daring, the next day!

When people speak, really listen and look them in the eye. Notice something you have not noticed about them before.

And choose at least one thing to do on this day that you used to love doing as a child.

LEARN FROM LITTLE PEOPLE

A very worthwhile exercise, tapping into how to feel more engaged in your life and the world around you, is to reflect back to being a child and what used to make you feel happy in the moment, no matter what others (especially your parents) thought.

To play is to be mindful—it is a return to a more natural and innocent state where our minds are absorbed in the task at hand and the 'monkey mind' is still. Play is not meant to have any purpose except to nourish joy and laughter. You don't have to take our word for it. The brilliant author of *Daring Greatly*, Brené Brown, is very keen on playing.

She told the *Huffington Post* that her family rethought their holidays together so that instead of sightseeing they could spend more time 'goofing off', walking, swimming, playing cards, 'things that make us all our most silly, creative, free-spirited selves'. There's a challenge to you all. Do you and your family really get a chance to play?

JANE SAYS:

When I was a child, I rearranged my room and 'spruced' it up every week or so. This was in between recording my own songs (lyrics by me) on an old tape recorder and practising them in front of the mirror with a hairbrush.

I remember once rescuing 'Banjo'—a poor baby sparrow who unfortunately fell from its nest. If you could die from too much love, I am pretty sure that is what Banjo ended up leaving this earth from—even though I tried my best to give him every chance of surviving, or so I thought.

I'm still not sure to this day that sparrows like peanut butter toast...

In short, I loved change, I loved writing and creating new things, and I loved caring for other people and living creatures as I believed life was precious. Although my life's journey has had its fair share of wrong turns, this still exactly represents what I am passionate about and what makes me happy today.

As well as finding a simple exercise like that enlightening—especially as, often, the things we love, and that make us feel more connected, comprise such a small percentage of what we actually spend our time doing—I have also slowly collected all the things little people say and/or do that actually are the keys to living a more mindful (and fun) life.

If you are anything like me, reading through the list is a reminder of how much we lose ourselves in what is not really important, and there are very simple ways we can connect more with ourselves and everything around us if we simply become more aware.

- It's OK to play on your own sometimes.
- When you feel something, just say it (as kindly as possible, of course).
- If you feel sad, cry. If you feel happy, laugh.
- Do one thing at a time.
- If you are not good at something, don't just give up—keep trying. It's actually how you get good at things (and feel pretty proud of yourself along the way).
- It's nice to nap.
- Tell people how amazing they are when you think or feel it.
- Draw not because you are a fine artist but because it is fun.
- It's OK to get mud on your clothes (it washes off).
- Hugs are the best.
- If something catches your eye, stop and investigate it. There's no real rush.
- Every day is an opportunity to learn something; even if small, it is still of value.
- Everyone has something important to share with you. Listen out for it.
- Share. It's not nice to be greedy.
- If you are mean to someone, you feel bad. There is a reason for that.
- Give love freely.
- It does not matter what people look like, you will always have something in common. Find it.
- Who says clothes have to match?
- Who says you even have to wear clothes?

Create a 'playlist':

List five ways you liked to play as a kid.

JAMES SAYS:

I have a lot of fun. At home, at work, out in the world, when we travel.

Hell, I even have fun on long commuting drives, just listening to my favourite music (The Flaming Lips, old Bob Dylan).

Here's my 'playlist' to start you off:

1. **Dressing up.**

2. **Climbing trees.**

3. **Making something out of nothing.**

4. **Digging in the mud** (preferably wet mud so a hot bubble bath post play was required).

5. **Making up funny plays or skits** and performing them to a jam-packed audience (that is, a lounge room comprising parents and, at best, one grandparent).

List five ways to bring play back into your life.

JAMES SAYS:

I am a person who unashamedly will want to stop the car near a beach or park and get out and play. It's as simple as that.

I love the fact that, for the most part, I have some flexibility to do that.

I am the biggest advocate for play—in children and adults, it is fundamental. Here are some thoughts on how to bring play back into your adult life:

1. **Be prepared to be silly.**

2. **Put your mobile phone away** (don't even use the excuse of capturing photos, because actual memories are better anyway).

3. **Get outdoors and away from screens.**

4. **Walk around in bare feet—lots.**

5. **Laugh out loud more often** (stop being a party-pooper).

'You can discover more about a person in an hour of play than in a year of conversation.'

—*Plato*
Philosopher and mathematician

From these little things, big things grow.

Another way to further cultivate connection with yourself and others is to think about (and express) what you are grateful for. Gratitude is a thankful appreciation for what you have received, whether tangible or intangible, and it helps people feel more positive emotions, savour positive experiences, deal with things that go wrong and build stronger relationships. In positive psychology research, gratitude is strongly and consistently associated with increased levels of happiness, and it is pretty easy to see why.

Psychologists from UC Davis and the University of Miami have done much of the research on gratitude. In one study, they asked all participants to write a few sentences each week, focusing on particular topics. One group wrote about things they were grateful for that had occurred during the week. A second group wrote about daily irritations or things that had displeased them, and the third wrote about events that had affected them (with no emphasis on them being positive or negative). After ten weeks, those who wrote about gratitude were more optimistic and felt better about their lives. Surprisingly, they also exercised more and had fewer visits to physicians than those who focused on sources of aggravation.

Another psychologist, at the University of Pennsylvania, tested the impact of various positive psychology interventions on 411 people, each compared with a control assignment of writing about early memories.

When their week's assignment was to write and personally deliver a letter of gratitude to someone who had never been properly thanked for his or her kindness, participants immediately exhibited a huge increase in happiness scores. This impact was greater than that from any other intervention, with benefits lasting for a month.

So how is gratitude related to being mindful? Well, it is a way for us to appreciate what we have instead of always reaching for the 'shiniest new thing' or feeling like we cannot be satisfied until every one of our insatiable needs have been met.

It helps us focus on the positive and take pleasure in the small things.

Some ways to practise gratitude on a regular basis include:

- **Keep a gratitude journal.** Make it a habit to write down or share with a friend or family member three things you are grateful for each day. Another great way to do this is as a family—we often go around the table at mealtime and share our 'three great things' for the day. It really helps, especially when you have had a bad day, to refocus on the positive.
- **Write thank-you notes.** This is a great thing to do at least once a month (or more often if you can manage it). It does not always have to be to someone you know well, and sometimes it is more fun if it isn't. It really is just to express your appreciation of that person's impact on your life—or other people's lives. You could send a note to someone you admire or to thank them for the good work they are doing for the world—that is the whole point, it doesn't always have to be about you!

EXERCISE
#18

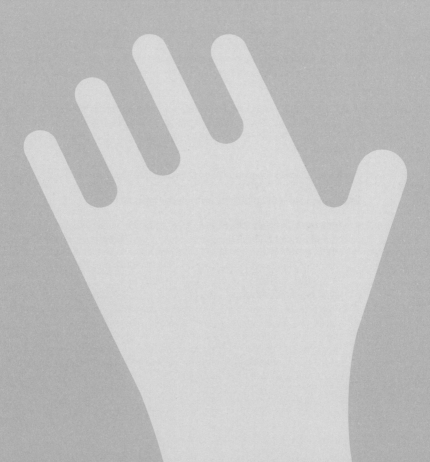

List the five things you're most grateful for at this present moment.

JAMES SAYS:

Here's my list of gratitude, to show you how it looks.

1

That I'm not born to war and poverty.

We live lives of absolute luxury. We need to remember that it's only by good fortune we've had a life of relative prosperity and joy, and as such we should do our best to show empathy and an open heart to our fellow men and women.

2

That I'm in good health.

You really don't notice your health until it's under threat. But we will all grow old and die, so it's a constant decline—and there ain't no point in thinking otherwise. Accept it, but also be grateful for health while you have it. Mindfulness brings respect for the body; it makes you consider what goes into your body and how that might either nurture or harm your health.

3

That I can contribute.

Education, cultural and social inheritance come with responsibility. I am deeply grateful for my life circumstances and also hold an unflinching view that people who can, must contribute to their communities. I also hope that Janey's and my journey can serve as a road map for other entrepreneurs who can bring their smarts, money and energy to social challenges and thus help make the world better.

4

That I know love.

I am grateful that I have people around me who love me, who each day provide support and let me be part of their world. Many are new faces who have come into my orbit in the last few years as I've evolved and become a kinder person myself. For me, it's crucial to nurture these new friendships, and I think too few people do it—familial relationships can destroy their own identities and they lose contact with others and are shut off from finding new friends.

5

That I allow myself free time.

I place a great emphasis on freedom, and despite the fact that I have a lot going on, I ensure that I have time to do nothing. The word 'busy' brings alarm bells to me. It's not badge of honour, and it can be a sign that you've entered the slipstream and lost control of your own life.

JANE SAYS:

Here's my list of gratitude, to show you how it looks.

1

Access to education.

We are so lucky to have the access to education that we do. I am extremely grateful for my own and am now constantly amazed and inspired by the education my boys experience from the dedicated teachers at our local school.

2

Passion.

This is a gift I am constantly grateful for. It has helped me speak up when I feel something is unjust, driven me towards new experiences, helped me find meaning in life and—most importantly—is what created Smiling Mind.

3 Courage.

It is hard not to feel scared, a lot of the time. So I am thankful for feeling and being courageous whenever I feel able to.

4 Holidays.

It is so important to recharge the batteries. My favourite holidays are the summer weekends in our simple, retro 'Chesney' caravan jammed in like sardines with sand all through our beds (if you can call them that!).

5 That I started meditating.

Without it I would not be who I am today, and Smiling Mind would not exist. I always laughed at the people with 'Magic Happens' stickers on their car. Now I don't (well, not as much anyway).

EXERCISE
#19

List five small things that bring you joy.

JAMES SAYS:

Here's my list of joy, to show you how it looks.

1 **Water.**
To look at the ocean brings a sense of timelessness to me. It reignites smells, feelings and emotions of childhood, and that brings deep joy.

2 **Sunshine.**
Sunshine makes me smile—it's not really any more complicated than that. It can be cold and sunny or hot and sunny, but without that sun, I'm always a little blue. I think many people are probably like this and maybe they've not fully understood it in themselves.

3 Happy people.

When I see someone with energy and very little ego, I am energised. It lifts the soul, it's contagious.

4 Lovers of life.

These people bring me joy. That zest for life might be expressed in art, in words, in science, in entrepreneurialism—it can be anything. There is an old man—in his mid-eighties—near my home and he walks at 7.15 am every day with fresh milk for his wife's tea, and once a week with a bunch of flowers. He wears rugby socks, but changes them so they are odd socks based on who will be playing the biggest game that week. This man has a love for life and that brings me joy.

5 The smile of a child.

We get lost in all our adult seriousness and hence risk creating a world whereby our children become like us—too focused on the future, too analytical about the past. When I see my wonderful children smile, having created something, worked something out, danced or just entered a happy moment, it brings me back to that joy.

JANE SAYS:

Here's my list of joy, to show you how it looks.

1

Passing by a florist and looking at what has been created from nature.

Not only am I blown away by nature's creativity but the artistic freaks who then make something I thought could get no better look even more spectacular.

2

Hearing other people laugh.

The best. Child or grown adult. Nothing more lifts the spirit than a LOL (aka 'laugh out loud'— not 'lots of love', which I once got caught out on).

3
Witnessing people being kind to strangers.

A true heart-warmer. I have seen a lot of this lately. People stopping to help someone who has fallen, offering to pay for someone's coffee if the cafe will not take a credit card or letting someone in an obvious hurry jump the queue. Simple but kind, it only takes a moment and usually costs nothing.

4
Hugging my dogs.

They're always so happy to see me, so soft and so grateful to have been saved from doggy death row thanks to Pet Rescue.

5
Seeing people singing in their car.

I absolutely love this. It makes me smile— and I am rather partial to it myself, so it is always a good reminder to crank the radio and not care who sees me.

Write a letter of gratitude to someone—whether you know them personally or not.

JAMES SAYS:

We've not met. I'm the tall bald guy who walks across the field in the morning when you are heading back from the shops.

I often have my kids with me and say hello. You might not know it but I wanted to let you know that you've always made me and my family smile.

Your energy has no ego, it pays no heed to judging those around you. I have seen you smile at the young Brazilian backpacker and I've seen you greet the building workers and the man in the fancy car. Maybe you don't know the impact you have but there is a caring harmony that you bring to the fellow walkers you meet on your morning travels.

Maybe I am romanticising things but I have always felt that you show in your spirit the tenderness and kindness that a man can have for his wife. The way you carry the precious flowers to your beloved partner rekindles my faith in marriage and the ability to keep lust and love alive.

Well, I wanted to say thank you for bringing a smile to my family and for having an open heart to the world.

FOCUS ON
WHAT IS TRULY
IMPORTANT

JANE SAYS:

You can Google anything these days.

As an incessant list- and goal-writer, I was having a field day one day and discovered a recommendation to write your own eulogy and epitaph. At first I thought this was perhaps the most insane thing I had ever seen—and that is coming from a person who loves being organised!

When I actually reflected on it, I realised it was the most perfect exercise to focus on what is truly important. If you had the chance to focus on one message people would receive when they walked past your gravestone, what would that be?

If someone was standing up in front of all the people most important to me, what would I hope they would say? Would anything I am spending the bulk of my time and energy on now even be mentioned in this speech?

Stay with me here. You see, I did go through with this exercise and, much like reflecting back on what I loved to do as a child, it reframed what was truly important to me and how I want to be in the world. I then shared it with those close to me and challenged them to keep me honest at all times and ensure I was on the right path so they could read it at my funeral—though maybe choose adults to share it with, as I think my children are probably still scarred from it!

Write your epitaph. What do you want it to say about you?

JANE SAYS:

So stop reading this and go do something.

Giving is living.

—Jane Martino

JAMES SAYS:

Charming and difficult, but beyond this he loved and was loved back.

—James Tutton

THAT'S IT,
FOLKS

One of the easiest and best ways to start a ten-minute daily practice is to use the Smiling Mind app and become part of the Smiling Mind community.

We created Smiling Mind as a not-for-profit initiative to enable as many people as possible all over the world to experience the benefits of mindfulness meditation.

The app is segmented into age groups so you can choose a tailored program, enter a few details and be off on your meditation journey. We have designed it to be implemented free of charge in schools across the nation, so we can embed this healthy habit into the fabric of our society, much like Physical Education has been. We like to think of it as 'PE for the mind', so it makes sense we have a vision for mindfulness to be on the Australian curriculum by 2020!

It is such an important, proactive mental health tool that all our future generations deserve to have it in their back pocket whenever they need it.

There is content relevant to individuals who want to start (or continue) their mindfulness journey, as well as guided programs for schools and community groups, all provided free of charge to ensure our goal of making mindfulness accessible to everyone is achieved.

The increased use of mindfulness meditation within the global sporting community also compelled us to work alongside specialised psychologists and experts from Cricket Australia and the Australian Football League to create a bespoke program for athletes, and release some of this content into our community for use in local sporting clubs.

The impact on the sporting field is emulated in the workplace—from the boardroom to the photocopier, use of this healthy, proactive tool is increasing productivity and relationships across some of the world's largest organisations. Smiling Mind is playing a significant role in the delivery of these programs well beyond the shores of Australia.

We are just two people who believe so intently in the importance of looking after your mind, we hope to give as many people as possible the gift that has made such a difference in our lives.

So we urge you to try it. Keep an open mind. If it is hard, like anything good in life, keep putting in the effort. The reward will not be a perfect life but instead the realisation that it is exactly the imperfection which makes it our very own, which helps us extract the wonder or cope with the roller-coaster ride life dishes out.

Either way, for ten minutes a day, who's in?

ACKNOWLEDGEMENTS

JANE SAYS:

This book is dedicated to my believers. There are a few, but perhaps not as many as you think. When James and I first came up with the concept of Smiling Mind, most people thought it was a crazy idea that would never work. See, the thing is, we did it anyway (obviously!). We all get served a large helping of doubt along life's journey, and not just from ourselves. I have had plenty and have made a distinct choice to ignore the noise and instead follow my heart and intuition - and surround myself with believers. People that see and understand me and all I have to offer the world—and love me for the ambitious, unique, sometimes immature and impulsive creature that I am. It makes life more fun—and makes far more magic happen because I keep these people close and they truly inspire me and spur me on when the chips are down.

So thank you to my ever-patient and supportive husband Matt who I am so grateful to, and who helped make my three little muses Tom, Henry and Sonny, who teach me how to be a better person every day—I love you all. To the believers that started it all, Mum and Dad, you are the best. And of course my ever-believing besties aka 'rocks' Mands, Stace, Chloe, Matty B, Bridge, Span, Leash and Jayne— love you long time xxx

JAMES SAYS:

For me this book is a product of many forces—both positive and negative. The positives are those many people who have shown support—first and foremost, my dear family and friends. The negative forces are grounded in the experience of losing those who are close and how this can serve to motivate us to prevent tragedy and loss.

To my son Cassius and daughter Harper—thanks for teaching me things and providing the ability for me to learn and know myself in a way I never expected.

To the team at Smiling Mind—thanks for giving blood, sweat and tears to making Janey's and my dream a reality. There is no road map for building a mindfulness meditation program like Smiling Mind but you have had the smarts to work it out and make it happen on the run.

To my parents—thanks for not giving me too much direction in life, which was a true gift because it let me work things out myself. From this I have been able to live a life that's based on the things that I value.

To my business partners—thanks for not once grumbling that I put my energies into Smiling Mind. The grace, charm and chivalry with which you've supported Janey's and my vision has been priceless.

To friends and to strangers—thanks for giving counsel, showing love, giving money, connecting new people, opening doors and generally helping. An old farmer with great heart and passion heard what we were doing and in our first phone conversation offered support on a very significant scale. He had faith that these two oddballs would come through and deliver on their dream. He did not have to write that cheque but he felt that the world would be a better place if he did. Thank you.

SCRIBBLE PAGES

Reading this book may inspire you to write down a few ideas and record your progress as you work through the first few weeks of your mindfulness meditation journey.

So here are a few scribble pages—for dreams, reflections and maybe some simple things to be grateful for.

Ten Minutes A Day For Ten Days

Date	Focus	Reflection

Published in 2016 by Hardie Grant Books

Hardie Grant Books (Australia)
Ground Floor, Building 1
658 Church Street
Richmond, Victoria 3121
www.hardiegrant.com.au

Hardie Grant Books (UK)
Dudley House, North Suite
34—35 Southampton Street
London WC2E 7HF
www.hardiegrant.co.uk

Cataloguing in publications data available from the National
Library of Australia

Smiling Mind
ISBN 978 1 74379 084 7

Cover and text design by Seesaw
Typeset in ConduitITC 9 pt
Printed and bound in China by 1010 Printing